AF076495

Angels
ALL AROUND US

Angels
ALL AROUND US

KAY HILTON
Illustrated by Julie Banks

XULON PRESS

Xulon Press
2301 Lucien Way #415
Maitland, FL 32751
407.339.4217
www.xulonpress.com

© 2020 by Kay Hilton

Illustrated by Julie Banks

All rights reserved solely by the author. The author guarantees all contents are original and do not infringe upon the legal rights of any other person or work. No part of this book may be reproduced in any form without the permission of the author. The views expressed in this book are not necessarily those of the publisher.

Unless otherwise indicated, Scripture quotations taken from the Holy Bible, New Living Translation (NLT). Copyright ©1996, 2004, 2007 by Tyndale House Foundation. Used by permission of Tyndale House Publishers, Inc.

Paperback ISBN-13: 978-1-6628-0310-9
Ebook ISBN-13: 978-1-6628-0311-6

DEDICATION

First, I dedicate this book to my husband Tom, who encouraged me throughout the entire process of writing this book. He is my biggest supporter and the love of my life. I finished writing this just before our fiftieth wedding anniversary.

Next, this book is dedicated to my son Scott and his wife Wendy, my daughter Erin and her husband William, and to my amazing grandchildren: Hannah, Noah, Ethan, John, Mary Grace, and Natalie. You fill my life with joy.

Last, but certainly not least, I dedicate this book to my Lord and Savior, Jesus Christ – the King of the World and the Ruler of the Angels!

Contents

Introduction   ix

One | What Are Angels?   1
Two | Types of Angels   11
Three | The Angel of the LORD   15
Four | Angels of Worship   19
Five | Messengers of Hope, Healing and Comfort   27
Six | Angels of Peace and Provision   35
Seven | Angels of Deliverance and Protection   45
Eight | The Business of Heaven   53
Nine | Activating Angels   63
Ten | Heaven on Earth   69

List of Contributors   75
About the Author   79
About the Illustrator   81

Introduction

I SEE ANGELS. THERE – I SAID IT! IT'S OUT THERE FOR ALL the world to see. I am not weird or strange – not too much, anyway. I am just an ordinary person who happens to see angels. Why do I see them? Simply because I asked. That's the only explanation I have. Angels are with me all the time because I invite them, and I ask the Lord to charge them to protect and assist me.

Before you get the wrong idea, let me clarify. Angels aren't just lounging in my living room, eating chips and dip, and watching television. But they are around – always on guard, keeping me from falling, worshiping with me, and bringing peace into my home.

To be honest, most of the time I don't actually even *see* my angels, but I know they are there. I might just sense their presence or see flashes of light. I sometimes hear music or smell a heavenly fragrance.

Until recently almost no one outside my immediate family knew about this. I wasn't hiding it; it just didn't come up very often. It's not something you just drop into a conversation: "Hey, I found this great new recipe for lasagna. And, by the way, I saw an angel today." Then God told me to write a book about angels. He has a way of stretching me beyond my comfort zone.

The Bible says that these wonderful spirit beings are God's messengers and servants. He sends them to care for His people (Heb. 1:14), and He orders them to protect His people (Ps. 91:11). There is no such promise for those who do not put their trust in the one true God; yet, because He is merciful, He does sometimes extend angelic care to unbelievers also.

We are NEVER to worship angels; and, indeed, they will not allow it (Rev. 19:1). Nor are we to pray to angels. However, it is appropriate to ask the Lord to release His angels to guard, protect, and minister to us as we live our lives in the service of our King.

Most (if not all) Christians have at some time been ministered to by an angel, quite likely without even knowing it. There are angels all around us. Have you barely missed being involved in an accident that was such a close call that you felt there must have been some divine intervention? Or perhaps you walked away from what should have been a fatal crash with hardly a scratch. Have you survived a tornado in the only part of the house that was left standing? We often refer to these events as *close calls* or *coincidences*; but chances are, they were angelic encounters.

Angels most often choose to remain behind the scenes, so as not to attract undue attention to themselves. But if you ask the Lord to open your spiritual eyes, you might sometimes see these heavenly helpers as they carry out their missions. Whether you see them or not, it is comforting to know that the Lord has commanded His angels to protect you and care for you. God has provided these supernatural helpers to assist you in carrying out His plan for your life.

As I am writing this, our world seems to be spinning out of control. We are struggling with a Coronavirus pandemic, riots and protests in our nation's streets, and anger directed at anyone who dares hold a differing opinion. Some might be tempted to think that the prince of the air and his fallen angels have control of the whole world. But in darkness, the Light shines brighter than ever. Jesus is the Lord of angel armies. He has never lost a battle, and He never will.

If you have never met Jesus, you can meet Him today. Each one of us was born with a condition called sin. We did not have to commit sin to be sinners. It was in our fleshly DNA, passed down from our ancestors

INTRODUCTION

Adam and Eve. That sin separated us from coming into the presence of Almighty God because He is completely holy. The only remedy was for a perfectly innocent person to die in our place as a sacrifice for our sin. But there was no one who was innocent.

Jesus, God's Son, being fully God, left the Father and became a man. He was conceived by the Holy Spirit in the body of a young virgin woman. He lived a totally sinless life and died on a cross, shedding His innocent blood as a once-and-for-all sacrifice for sin for all who would believe on Him. Anyone who accepts Jesus' offer of salvation is born again into the kingdom of God and will live with Jesus forever (John 3:16). Meeting ten thousand angels could never compare with meeting Jesus, the One who created the angels and is Lord of all creation. If you have not made the decision to entrust your life and your eternal future to Him, please do not wait another moment.

Dear Jesus, I believe that you are the Son of the living God. Thank you for taking my place on the cross; for dying and shedding your blood to pay the penalty for my sins. Thank you for clothing me in your righteousness and making me new. Father God, thank you for accepting me as your child. Holy Spirit, guide me and fill me with the power to live this new life. Lord, give me spiritual eyes to see and spiritual ears to hear. In the mighty Name of Jesus. Amen.

One

WHAT ARE ANGELS?

God calls his angels messengers swift as the wind, and servants made of flaming fire. **Heb. 1:7**

But angels are only servants. They are spirits sent from God to care for those who will receive salvation. **Heb. 1:14**

ANGELS. WHAT COMES TO MIND WHEN YOU HEAR THAT word? Cute chubby babies with little wings sprouting from their backs? Or the delicate winged lady in an elegant gown who gazes serenely from atop your Christmas tree?

For centuries artists have attempted to depict angels in paintings and sculptures. Most of those artistic renderings, while often beautiful, have only added to the misconceptions about angels.

Much of what is believed about these marvelous supernatural creatures is not true. Angels are not mythical creatures or characters from fairy tales. They are real beings. We find them present and active in the Bible from Genesis to Revelation. They move effortlessly between the supernatural and the natural (or earthly) realms as they carry out the commands of the Most High God. We will look to the Bible for the truth about angels– who they are, what they do and how we can properly interact with these heavenly helpers.

Not only were angels engaged in the lives of men and women of Bible times; they are still working to assist mankind today. I will share a few of my personal experiences with angels in this book, along with those of others who have had angelic encounters. We will learn more about these angels all around us.

Before God created mankind, He already had a plan and purpose for each one of us. Although we have free will and can resist or even fully rebel against God's plan, God's heart is for us to choose the destiny for which we were created. He has charged His angels to assist us in fulfilling our destinies. Angels do this in numerous ways. They help protect from both physical and demonic attacks. They engage in spiritual warfare. They bring messages, provision, or healing from God. They even perform miracles at God's command.

In most cases, angels do their work invisibly. They remain hidden from human view unless it is necessary for them to be seen for them to complete their missions. Even then, often they will appear as ordinary human beings. They will offer little information about themselves–usually not even their names. They complete their missions quickly; then they are gone. Only later–sometimes much later–do humans realize that they had been in the presence of a heavenly helper.

The word **angel** comes from the Greek *angelos* (Strong's Concordance G32), meaning *messenger*. The Hebrew word that is most often translated as **angel** is *mal'ak* (Strong's Concordance H4397), also meaning *messenger* or *sent one*. Angels are mentioned over three hundred times in the Bible. Other terms are used in the Bible to refer to these celestial beings as well.

OTHER WORDS FOR ANGELS IN THE BIBLE

- sons of God (Gen. 6:2, 4; Job 1:6, 38:7; Ps. 89:6)
- heavenly hosts (Ps. 103:21, 148:2; Luke 2:13)
- chariots (2 Kgs. 6:17; Ps. 68:17; Zech. 6:1-6)
- sons of the Most High (Ps. 82:6)

- watchers (Dn. 4:13, 17, 23-24)
- holy ones (Dn. 4:13, 17; Ps. 89:5, 7, 148:5; Jude 14-15)
- gods (Ps. 82:1,6)
- morning stars (Job 39:7; Rev. 12:4)
- divine assembly/council (Ps. 82:1; Ps. 89:5, 7)
- ministering spirits (Heb. 1:14)

FROM WHERE DID ANGELS COME?

Angels are spirit beings and were created by God, through and for Christ.

Christ is the one through whom God created everything in heaven and earth. He made the things we can see and the things we can't see–kings, kingdoms, rulers, and authorities. Everything has been created through Him and for Him. **Col. 1:16**

Angels are God's family in the spirit realm, created to live with Him and carry out His commands. They are called sons of God, sons of the Most High, even gods; yet angels are not equal to God. Angels have been around a long time. In the Old Testament, God told Job that the angels sang and shouted for joy when He created the earth.

Where were you when I laid the foundations of the earth? Tell me if you know so much. Do you know how its dimensions were determined and who did the surveying? What supports its foundations, and who laid its cornerstone as the morning stars sang together and all the angels shouted for joy? **Job 38:4-7**

Angels have been witnesses to all of man's history. And they have been active in much more of it than we realize.

ANGELS WERE CREATED TO PRAISE AND WORSHIP GOD.

Some angels are continuously praising and worshipping Almighty God around His throne in heaven.

And then, when he presented his honored Son to the world, God said, "Let all the angels of God worship Him." **Heb. 1:6**

*Day after day and night after night they keep on saying, "Holy, holy, holy is the Lord God Almighty—the one who always was, who is, and who is still to come." * **Rev. 4:8**

And all the angels were standing around the throne and around the elders and the four living beings. And they fell face down before the throne and worshiped God. They said, "Amen! Blessing and glory and wisdom and thanksgiving and honor and power and strength belong to our God forever and ever. Amen!" **Rev. 7:11-12**

ANGELS ARE SERVANTS OF GOD.

Angels take orders from the Lord. He commands them to carry messages, to serve, guard and protect humans, to fight enemies, and even to carry out judgment.

God calls his angels messengers swift as the wind, and servants made of flaming fire. **Heb. 1:7**

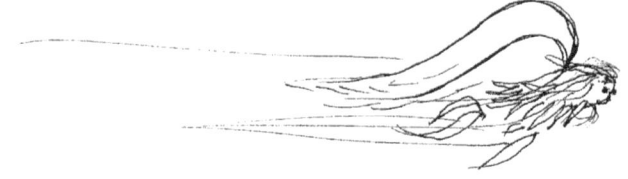

HOW MANY ANGELS EXIST?

We cannot know how many angels there are, for the Bible says that there are too many to count.

No, you have come to Mount Zion, to the city of the living God, the heavenly Jerusalem, and to thousands of angels in joyful assembly. **Heb. 12:22**

Then I looked again, and I heard the singing of thousands and millions of angels around the throne and the living beings and the elders. **Rev. 5:11**

ANGELS ARE NOT TO BE WORSHIPPED.

When an angel appears to a mortal, it may induce a range of emotions, from incredulous wonder to knee-shaking fear; but angels are never to be worshiped. When a human has erroneously started to worship an angel, the angel has corrected the person.

And don't let anyone say you must worship angels, even though they say they have had visions about this. These people claim to be so humble, but their sinful minds have made them proud.

Col. 2:18

Then I fell down at his feet to worship him, but he said, "No, don't worship me. For I am a servant of God, just like you and other brothers and sisters who testify of their faith in Jesus. Worship God. For the essence of prophecy is to give a clear witness for Jesus."

Rev. 19:10

I, John, am the one who saw and heard all these things. And when I saw and heard these things, I fell down to worship the angel who showed them to me. But again he said, "No, don't worship me. I am a servant of God, just like you and your brothers the prophets, as well as all who obey what is written in this scroll. Worship God!"

Rev. 22:8-9

Humans are never to worship or pray to angels.

DO ANGELS DIE?

Angels are immortal spirit beings; therefore, they do not age, get sick, or die. They were created as adults, so there are no baby angels waiting to grow up and earn their wings.

The winds are your messengers; flames of fire are your servants.

Ps. 104:4

And they will never die again. In these respects they are like angels.

Luke 20:36

DO ANGELS MARRY IN HEAVEN?

As immortal spirit beings, angels do not need to marry or have children in heaven to perpetuate their kind.

For when the dead rise, they won't be married. They will be like the angels in heaven.

Mt. 22:30

WHAT KIND OF BODIES DO ANGELS HAVE?

An angel is a pure spirit being without a natural or physical body, yet with a discernable form. Technically, as a pure spirit, an angel has no gender. In the Bible, angels are most often referred to as male. However, in Zechariah 5:9, we find two female winged spirits.

When ministering to humans, angels may appear in spirit form or they may manifest in a physical human body, either male or female. They might even appear as an animal, although they are not bound or limited by a physical body of any kind. Many times, an angel will look so much like an ordinary human that the person who encounters the heavenly messenger will not realize that he or she has been in the presence of an angel until afterwards.

***Don't forget to show hospitality** to strangers, for some who have done this have entertained angels without realizing it!* **Heb. 13:2**

DO ANGELS EAT?

Yes. The Bible indicates that the manna which God rained down from heaven to feed the Hebrew people in the wilderness was "angel food."

But he commanded the skies to open–he opened the doors of heaven–and rained down manna for them to eat. He gave them bread from heaven. They ate the food of angels! God gave them all they could hold. **Ps. 78:23-25**

When three heavenly visitors appeared to Abraham at the oaks of Mamre, Abraham asked them to wait while a meal was prepared. The three visitors waited and shared a meal with Abraham, which consisted of meat, curds, and milk (Gen. 18:1-8). The two angels that were sent to Lot in Sodom went into his house and ate a meal (Gen. 19:1-3). While the Bible does not make it clear if angels *must* eat, it does indicate that they *can*.

DO ANGELS HAVE WINGS?

Some angels have wings, but many do not. A type of angel called a *seraph* (plural *seraphim*) has six wings (Isa. 6:2). *Cherubs* (plural *cherubim*) may have four wings (Eze. 1:8, 10:20-21). Other angels may have two wings or no wings at all.

The angels that have wings were created with wings; they do not have to earn them. Although it made for good drama, the idea that a ringing bell means an angel is getting his wings originated in Hollywood rather than heaven. Sorry, Clarence! Even angels without any wings at all appear to be able to "fly" or move rapidly from one place to another without effort.

And I saw another angel flying through the heavens, carrying the Good News to preach to the people who belong to this world—to every nation, tribe, language and people.

Rev. 14:6

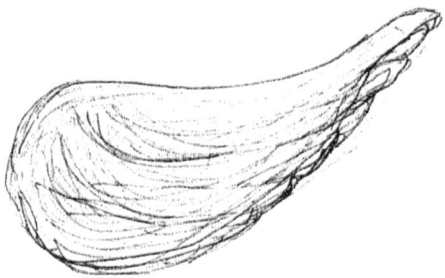

DO PEOPLE BECOME ANGELS WHEN THEY DIE?

Contrary to popular myth, people do not become angels when they die. Humans are spirit beings in physical bodies. They were created as humans and always will be human. They will never become angels, nor will they receive wings in heaven.

God created an uncountable number of angels before He created the earth; and since they never die, we do not have to worry that God might take one of our loved ones because of a shortage of angels.

When Christians die, they go to heaven to be with the Lord; but they do not become angels. They will live as spirit beings; *like* angels, in that they will each have a pure spiritual "body" which has form and is recognizable and is free from the limitations of a natural body. But people will always be people, and angels will always be angels.

Yes, we are fully confident, and we would rather be away from these bodies, for then we will be at home with the Lord. **2 Cor. 5:8**

At the Rapture (the first Resurrection], believers will receive their immortal physical bodies. Until then, believers in heaven will function quite well in spirit form.

ANGELS ARE SUBJECT TO JESUS.

Jesus has absolute power over every angel, both now and in the future.

Now Christ has gone to heaven. He is seated in the place of honor next to God, and all the angels and authorities and powers are bowing before him.

1 Pet. 3:22

This is the same mighty power that raised Christ from the dead and seated him in the place of honor at God's right hand in the heavenly realms. Now he is far above any ruler or authority or power or leader or anything else in this world or in the world to come.

Eph. 1:19-21

Heavenly Father, thank you for the gift of salvation through your Son Jesus. Jesus, I believe in you and I thank you for saving me from my sins and giving me eternal life. I want to love you and serve you forever. I want to participate in your Kingdom work on the earth. Thank you for assigning angels to assist me and minister to me as I follow your will and your way for my life. I give you permission to correct any misconceptions or misunderstandings I have had about angels. Holy Spirit, teach me and guide me into all truth. In the mighty Name of Jesus, Amen!

Two

Types of Angels

For who in all of heaven can compare with the LORD? What mightiest angel is anything like the LORD? **Ps. 89:6**

THE BIBLE INDICATES THAT THERE ARE DIFFERENT types of angels with varying positions of rank and authority. Many theologians over the centuries have placed angels in a hierarchy scale consisting of three spheres or choirs, which are each also divided into three types, in descending order or rank. Jesus is the ruler of the angels and they are all subject to Him.

Just a word of caution is appropriate about angel types. Although these types, with some variations, have been generally agreed upon by many Bible scholars for a long time, we must not limit God. When we get to heaven, I am certain that we will find many, many surprises, so we should not be too dogmatic about types of angels.

CAUTION: Although angels are glorious, they do not compare with the glory of God. We are forbidden to worship or pray to angels for any reason. They were created to serve and worship God and to minister to humans.

JESUS

Now he is far above any ruler or authority or power or leader **or** *anything else in this world or in the world* **to** *come.* **Eph 1:21**

<u>1st Sphere</u>: These angels serve as heavenly servants of God and are always in His presence, surrounding His throne.

1. Seraphim–Isa. 6:1-8 – These are the angels that are closest to God. Seraphim means *burning ones*. They continuously praise the Lord and protect His throne. They are fiery six-winged beings with two wings that cover their faces, two wings that cover their feet, and two wings that are used to fly. They are aflame with the glory of God. They continually surround the throne of God, singing praises to Him.

2. Cherubim – Eze. 10:1-22–This class of angels is the second closest to God. They are associated with the glory of God and they defend His holiness. This type of angel might include the four "living creatures" or "living beings" who each have four faces and four wings covered with eyes (although Rev. 4:8 describes four living creatures with six wings). Some cherubim may have human-like bodies. Cherubim guarded the entrance to the garden of Eden after the fall. Images of cherubim were carved on the lid of the Ark of the Covenant and were used to decorate the temple of God.

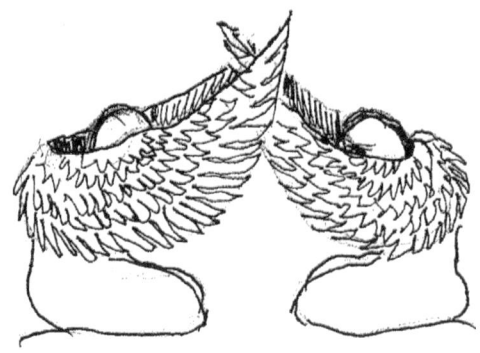

3. Thrones/Ophanim – Col. 1:16–Some scholars believe these are angels that sit on thrones and dispense God's judgment (for example, the 24 Elders). They are a symbol of God's justice and authority. Others think these are the Ophanim, the many-eyed wheels associated with the cherubim.

2<u>nd</u> Sphere: These angels work as heavenly governors of the creation. They are concerned with the functions of the universe.

4. Dominions –Eph. 1:21; Col. 1:16 – These are angels of leadership and justice. They minister divine order in the universe and regulate the duties of lower angels. They rarely make themselves known to humans.

5. Virtues/Strongholds – Eph. 1:21 – These are angels through which signs and wonders are performed at God's command. They have supernatural strength and energy. They are encouragers and motivators.

6. Powers/Authorities – Eph. 3:10 – These are warrior angels. They oppose evil spirits, holding back wicked attacks and strategies of the enemy against God's people. They are continuously at war against the forces of evil. They may appear in full battle dress, having both offensive and defensive weapons.

3rd Sphere: These angels serve as heavenly guides, guardians, protectors, and messengers to humans. These are the angels that are all around us.

7. Principalities/Rulers – Eph. 3:10 – These angels preside over regions, nations, kingdoms, and churches. They often appear dressed in garments which represent the culture of the nation or region to which they are assigned. Others may appear wearing a crown and carrying a scepter. They inspire art, science, and culture. They preside over bands of angels and charge them with carrying out their ministries.

8. Archangels – 1 Thess. 4:16; Jude 1:9 – These are "Head" or "Chief" angels. The only archangel specifically mentioned by name in the Bible is Michael, who is assigned to protect Israel. Many scholars believe that Gabriel could also be an archangel because he said that he stands in the very presence of God (see Luke 1:19), and because he was commissioned to deliver news of the births of both John the Baptist and Jesus the Messiah.

9. Ministering Spirits/Angels – Genesis through Revelation – These are the angels that interact most with humans. Guardian angels come from this class of angels. This class of angels includes angels of comfort, protection, healing, deliverance, provision, and miracles, as well as messenger angels. They usually appear in human form.

Creator God, you do all things well. I am amazed by the diversity of angelic beings that you have created. Yet these glorious ones pale in comparison to your glory! Thank you for sending angels to minister to me, protect me, and help me as I serve you in the things you have ordained for me to do. Release your angels to come alongside me as I fulfill the purposes you have determined for me. In the Precious Name of Jesus! Amen.

Three

The Angel of the LORD

For the angel of the LORD guards all who fear him, and he rescues them.
Ps. 34:7

The Angel of the LORD appeared throughout the Old Testament. In some instances, this mysterious being seemed to be a pre-incarnate manifestation of Christ, because He said or did things that could only be attributed to God, as seen in the following examples (underline mine).

To Abraham: *Then the Angel of the LORD called again to Abraham from heaven, "This is what the LORD says: Because you have obeyed me and have not withheld even your beloved son, <u>I swear by my own self</u> that <u>I will bless you</u> richly. <u>I will multiply your descendants</u> into countless millions, like the stars of the sky and the sand on the seashore. They will conquer their enemies, and through your descendants, all the nations of the earth will be blessed–all because you have obeyed me."]*

Gen. 22:15-18

To Jacob: *Then in my dream the Angel of God said to me, "Jacob!" And I replied. "Yes, I'm listening!" The angel said, "Look and you will see* *that only the streaked, speckled, and spotted males are mating with the females of your flock. For I have seen all that Laban has done to you. <u>I am the God you met at Bethel</u>, the place where you anointed the pillar of stone and made a vow to serve me. Now leave this country and return to the land you came from."*

Gen. 31:11-13

To Moses: **Suddenly, the angel of the LORD appeared to him as a blazing fire in a bush. Moses was amazed because the bush was engulfed in flames, but it didn't burn up. "Amazing!" Moses said to himself. "Why isn't that bush burning up? I must go over to see this."**

<u>**When the LORD saw that he had caught Moses' attention, God called to him from the bush,**</u> **"Moses, Moses!"**

Ex. 3:2-4

In examples such as these, the Angel of the LORD equates Himself with God by word or deed, so we must conclude that He is the preincarnate Jesus, manifesting in a human body before He was born in the flesh. This is called a *theophany*. This does NOT mean that Jesus is an angel. Jesus is far greater than the angels; and indeed, the angels were created by Him and through Him (Heb. 1:4; Col. 1:16).

THE ANGEL OF THE LORD

In the New Testament, we find *an* angel of the Lord, but not *the* Angel of the LORD. This angel could not be the pre-incarnate Jesus, because he appears *after* Jesus was conceived or born.

An angel of the Lord confirmed the virgin Mary's story to her betrothed husband Joseph, telling Joseph not to be afraid to marry Mary, for the baby was indeed conceived by the Holy Spirit (Matt. 1:20).

An angel of the Lord announced the birth of Jesus to a group of shepherds as they watched over their flocks in the fields at night. Then he was joined by a multitude of heavenly hosts who were praising God along with him (Luke 2:8-14).

After the wise men visited the child Jesus, an angel of the Lord appeared to Joseph in a dream telling him to take Mary and Jesus and flee to Egypt because King Herod was going to search for the child to destroy him (Matt. 2:13-14). Joseph heeded the angel's warning. He got up immediately and escaped to Egypt with Mary and Jesus during the night. Later, the angel appeared to Joseph again in a dream and told him to move his family back to Israel (Matt. 2:19-22).

An angel of the Lord enabled Peter's escape from prison on the night before King Herod planned to execute him (Acts 12:6-10). Shortly after Peter's escape, an angel of the Lord struck King Herod with a terrible malady and he died, because He allowed the people to give him glory that was due only to God (Acts 12:21- 24).

In each of these New Testament examples, the angel of the Lord appears to be an incredibly special angel who works on God's behalf–but only an angel – not God Himself. We do not even know if it was the same angel every time. All angels are under God's authority and He commands them to do as He wills. What we can see very clearly is that God uses His angels to carry out His plans and purposes in the lives of humans.

Lord Jesus, I acknowledge that you are the Creator and Sustainer of all things, including the angels. You are the Lord of Hosts–the Ruler of all the Angels. I thank you for all the times that you have commanded angels to assist me when I was unaware. Forgive me for calling "coincidence" what you provided for me. Make me more discerning of your assistance in the form of your heavenly host, that I may give you proper honor and glory. For you are worthy of all praise! Amen.

Four

Angels of Worship

Praise the LORD! Praise the LORD from the heavens! Praise him from the skies! Praise him, all his angels! Praise him, all the armies of heaven!
Ps. 148:1-2

THE BOOK OF DANIEL REFERS TO CERTAIN ANGELS AS *watchers* or *observers*. Scripture indicates that angels do indeed observe God's people with interest. When the apostle Paul wrote to the church at Corinth about the example of humility being modeled by the apostles, he said, *"But sometimes I think God has put us apostles on display, like prisoners of war at the end of a victor's parade, condemned to die. We have become a spectacle to the entire world–to people and to angels alike."*

1 Cor. 4:9

In Paul's letter to Timothy regarding how to conduct ministry in an honorable way, Paul wrote, *"I solemnly command you in the presence of God and Christ Jesus and the holy angels to obey these instructions without taking sides or showing special favor to anyone"* (**1 Tim. 5:21**). It is apparent that the apostle Paul believed that angels were watching the activities of God's people, and he was calling on them to bear witness to his charge to Timothy.

Peter wrote about the prophets of old who had glimpses of the Messiah whose suffering would bring salvation to the people and glory to God. These ancient prophets questioned when these things would happen, but it was revealed to them that they were prophesying about this mystery for later generations that were not yet born. This salvation was so amazing that the apostle Peter went on to say, *"It is all so wonderful that even the angels are eagerly watching these things happen."*

1 Pet. 1:12

Jesus Himself said, *"In the same way, there is joy in the presence of God's angels when even one sinner repents."*

Luke 15:10

Imagine that. The angels have a celebration every time someone is born into the kingdom of God. It is obvious that angels are indeed watching or observing the activities of humans on earth, and even interacting with them.

One of the most delightful ways that angels interact with humans is during times of praise and worship. Since angels were created to praise and worship Almighty God, it makes perfect sense that they are attracted to humans who are doing the same. Sometimes they even join in. There have been reports of the sound of angel voices singing along with worshippers. Sometimes angels play musical instruments during times of worship, occasionally even continuing the music after the humans have stopped.

Many years ago, I asked God to increase my discernment and my spiritual vision. I thanked Him for surrounding me with angels to protect me and help me every day. It wasn't that I needed to see angels to build my faith, but if the Lord was making this heavenly assistance available, then I wanted to cooperate and increase my discernment. I invited the angels that I knew were around me to join in my private worship time.

Angels began to show up when I prayed or worshipped in my home. Now I sense their presence almost continually. Sometimes I see flashes of light or color flying through the room or past my windows. Other times I hear beautiful music–sometimes just voices, sometimes just instruments, and other times both. Often there is suddenly a heavenly fragrance in the air, with no natural explanation.

Although I have been interacting with angels for a long time, only a very few people knew this about me until shortly before I started writing this book. There are a couple of reasons why I kept it to myself. If you start telling people you see angels, some of them think you are crazy. But more importantly, I did not want to give the impression that I exalt angels in any way. Angels are glorious, but they only reflect the glory of God, just as we should do. Angels are my friends and helpers, but no angel ever died for my sins. Only Jesus did that.

Being hospitable to angels is not praying to them. Inviting them to worship with you is not prayer. People had conversations with angels in the Bible almost every time they encountered one, so obviously, talking to an angel is not prohibited.

I welcome angels into my home every day. They go with me wherever I go. My angels are always around me. When my husband and I travel, I ask the Lord to assign extra angels to surround us, and others to protect our home, our pets, and belongings while we are away.

THE ANGEL ALERT

We live in a rural area, so I purchased a driveway alert a year or so ago for extra security. It made a sound like a doorbell chime whenever someone drove up the little dead-end road to our house. Our dog soon learned that it meant visitors were coming and she would bark every time it went off.

Before long we noticed that the alarm was going off frequently when there was no movement on the road. We didn't figure it out until I happened to look out my window one morning as I was trying to read my Bible to the frequent alarms and barking. There were angels flying around our yard, setting off the alarm! From then on, we called it the "Angel Alert." We finally had to deactivate the alarm. God has a sense of humor. He let me know that He was taking care of security at our house by placing angels all around us.

I am just an ordinary person. I am not special or well-known, but God loves me, and He assigns angels to me. He does the same for you. Just ask the Lord to sharpen your spiritual vision. You might be amazed at what you see. There are angels all around you.

ANGELS SING ALONG

At our church on either side of the front platform were small, enclosed areas which extended out onto the platform itself. The enclosure on the right housed the drums, while the left enclosure hid the back stairs to the platform. During worship I occasionally saw angels sitting or standing on top of these areas, singing along with the worshippers. Sometimes they even danced with joy during the praise songs. A few times I only heard their voices without seeing them.

These angels were about ten feet tall, dressed in shining, white garments: sometimes in simple robes and other times in pants with a tunic top. I have seen as few as two or as many as four at a given time. I could not see details of their faces because they were so high up in the building and there was a brilliant glow that surrounded them. They did not join the services often, but when they did grace us with their presence, it was when the worship was passionate. The musical ability of the people who played, sang, or led worship did not seem to matter.

Worship angels respond to the pure intent of hearts that seek to bring glory and honor to God. When you praise and worship God with a hunger for His presence, angels are watching and are eager to participate. Angels are all around us.

ANGELS AT CHILDREN'S CHURCH

Marla describes a visitation by an angel: "About 2015, my husband Scott and I were ministering at a small church in Brazil. During the praise and worship, we looked up and saw a brilliant, shining angel beside the door to the room where the children were. I took a picture; not even sure if it would show up. Then I asked the angel what he was doing, and he said, 'Keeping watch over the children.'

"After the service we were talking to the pastors and I decided to show them the picture. They got all excited and told us (through an interpreter) that before every service they pray over the children's room and pray for angels to stand guard over it. They were so excited to see that their prayers were working!"

ANGELS IN THE PRAYER CLOSET

Retha had an office in her house that had become her prayer closet. Every morning she prayed and worshiped God in that little office, sometimes for hours on end; especially when she was going through difficult times.

One morning as Retha sang to the Lord, she became aware of the presence of angels in the room with her. She could neither see nor hear them, but she knew for certain that they were there. She said, "That office was full of angels, worshipping with me at the throne of God."

CABIN ANGELS (name changed)

Nita went to her cabin in the woods of South Mississippi one morning to spend some time alone with the Lord. This little one-room cabin was where she and God spent many hours together. Hidden deep in the woods and accessible only by a dirt trail, it was built high off the ground to protect it from the rising waters of the creek its front balcony overlooked. It was here that Nita could bare her soul to her Lord–singing, praying, laughing, crying, and studying His Word.

At a Spiritual Life Conference that Nita had recently attended, the speaker had taught some sessions about angels. He had said that it is good to thank God for the ways that His angels minister to us, even though we may be unaware of their services. He had said that it was even appropriate to thank those angels when we sense they are near. So, as Nita praised and worshiped God, pouring out her heart and expressing her love for Him, she remembered to thank the Lord for sending angels to minister to her throughout her life–angels of worship, comfort, healing, protection, etc.

As Nita thanked the Lord for sending those heavenly helpers, she became aware of the presence of angels all around the cabin. As she sang and prayed, the angels would gather close and watch through the windows. She said a quiet "Thank you" to them. She sensed that they were saying "Thank you" back to her. It was a precious time as Nita continued to worship the Lord, surrounded by the angels.

Evidently the Lord had a special fondness for that little cabin. About a year after that encounter, Hurricane Katrina ravaged the Gulf Coast, with damage extending more than a hundred miles inland where the cabin was located. It was weeks before Nita's husband could clear the path enough to walk back to the cabin. The cabin was surrounded by trees, with one enormous oak tree right beside the stairs that went up to the entrance.

When they finally were able to check for damages, they found extraordinarily little harm had been done to the cabin. The giant tree, once completely straight, was bent over at an odd angle. It wasn't broken–only the trunk was bent over. If it had fallen or broken, it would have destroyed the cabin. Nita looked at the strange sight and wondered, "Lord, what happened to this tree?" The Lord immediately answered, "My angel had his hand on it." It looked exactly like a large hand had bent it over. When Nita told her husband what she had heard, he just said, "Makes sense to me!"

THE LAUGHING ANGEL

Pat was at a worship service in Texas where the keyboard player was gifted in the ability to usher in the glory of the Lord. There was much freedom to worship in the service and the presence of the Lord was especially joyful. It became obvious that angels were joining the worship. Pat was spinning and dancing before the Lord when she suddenly lost her balance and fell – right onto her angel! She could hear him laughing. Later in the service, while she was just standing still and soaking in the music, Pat felt an angel wing brush across her cheek. There was much joy in worshipping the Lord along with the angels.

ANGELS AT AN ANGEL CONFERNCE

A well-documented angelic encounter occurred in Nashville, TN, when about 120 people were gathered for the final session of the Methodist School for the Supernatural. One of the speakers at this event was author, artist, and teacher Kevin Basconi, who had been teaching about angels.

Evangelist Ric Wright of Resurrection Lifestyle Ministries recalls it this way: "As the session was coming to a close, Kevin was walking around the room when he stopped in front of me and said, 'I think God wants you to do something.' Then he handed me the microphone. Well, I didn't have a clue what to do, so I just started singing in the Spirit. About fifteen to twenty people joined in, mostly female; and as I was the only one with a microphone, mine was about the only male voice being heard. Suddenly, about sixty male voices joined in the singing; and in the Spirit, we could see angels encircling the room. Kevin asked us to be quiet, and the angels continued to sing for about thirty-five minutes."

Lord, you are worthy of all honor and glory and praise! It is my great pleasure to worship you. I welcome your angels to join me as I praise you. Let everything that has breath praise your Holy Name! Amen.

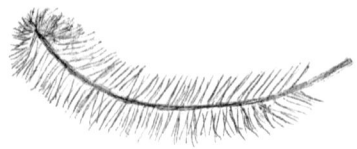

Five

Messengers of Hope, Healing, and Comfort

God calls his angels messengers swift as the wind, and servants made of flaming fire. **Heb. 1:7**

GOD HAS USED ANGELS TO DELIVER MESSAGES MANY times. Angels delivered the law (the commandments) to Moses (Acts 7:53). An angel gave Philip directions to take a certain road, which led him to an encounter with the eunuch from Ethiopia. The eunuch received the Good News about Jesus from Philip; then he believed and was baptized (Acts 8:26-38).

Cornelius, a Roman army officer, received a message from an angel that he should send some men to Joppa to find a man named Simon Peter. Then they were to extend to him an invitation to visit Cornelius at his home in Caesarea. As a result of that visit, the whole gentile household believed in Jesus, received the Holy Spirit, and were baptized (Acts 10).

An angel confirmed to Joseph that Mary was pregnant by the Holy Spirit and that the child was to be called Jesus (Matt. 1:19-21). Angels announced the birth of Jesus to a group of shepherds in the fields outside Bethlehem (Luke 2:8-14}. Angels informed the women at the empty tomb that Jesus was alive and instructed them to go and tell the disciples (Matt. 28:5-7, Mark 16:5-8, Luke 24:4-7). An angel delivered healing to those who stepped into the waters of the pool of Bethsaida (John 5:4).

The most well-known messenger angel is Gabriel. In the Old Testament, he interpreted visions and brought answers to the prophet Daniel's prayers (Dan. 8:15-27; 9:20-27). In the New Testament, Gabriel told Zechariah that he and his wife Elizabeth would have a baby and they were to name him John. This child would later come to be called John the Baptist, the one who prepared the way for Jesus the Messiah (Luke 1:11-19). The same angel Gabriel announced to the young virgin Mary that she would become pregnant by the Holy Spirit and give birth to Jesus, the long-awaited Messiah (Luke 1:26-38).

Most messenger angels today do not give their names, but they deliver messages to God's people just the same. Let's look at a few modern-day examples of angels all around us.

ANGELS BRING NEWS OF AN ACCIDENT

Lydia and her husband left after work on Friday evening, July 3, 1992, taking their three daughters on a vacation from Mississippi to Florida to experience Disney World. Her sister Kay, brother-in-law Rick and their children were waiting for them some miles ahead at the Florida Welcome Center, the first Rest Area after crossing the Florida state line on the Interstate. They had planned to meet and ride alongside each other to Tampa where they would stay with a relative during the vacation.

Tragically, Lydia's family never made it to the Rest Area. Their car was struck head-on by a drunk driver going the wrong way on the interstate at high speed, killing Lydia's husband Darby on impact, along with the driver of the other vehicle.

At the Rest Area, Rick and Kay's family was waiting on the farthest side away from the entrance, because the place was so crowded due to Fourth of July traffic. They were notified of the accident by two of God's messenger angels, who appeared as an elderly couple.

Rick remembers: "They pulled into the Rest Area–a man and a woman. They drove straight up to us and asked if we were waiting for someone. I said, 'Yes.' They told us about the accident and said we should go check it out. Then they left. They did not get out to use the bathroom or stretch their legs. They had no reason to pull into the Rest Area; and they did not speak to anyone else. That's what made me drive back to check it out."

Kay said the same thing, but she emphasized that the couple gave a description of everyone in the accident, including approximate age, gender and even hair color. She added, "That side of the interstate was closed because of the bad wreck, but somehow they got through and pulled into the Rest Area. The Rest Area was packed because it was Fourth of July weekend, but they passed the other people and drove straight up to us – only us."

Rick and Kay and their children drove back to the scene of the accident and Rick was able to identify the family to the authorities. Sadly, after nine hours of surgery, five-year-old Becky passed away. Seventeen-year-old Jennifer was hospitalized only a few days for minor injuries. Fourteen-year-old Misty was able to go home after several surgeries and six months of therapy. Doctors thought that even if Lydia survived, she would never speak or walk or function normally due to severe head trauma and other multiple injuries. But God had other plans. After eight months of therapy, she, too, went home. God continued to heal her body and restore her soul.

Note from Author: Just a couple of years after the accident, Lydia remarried. My husband Tom and I had the honor of singing at her wedding. It was also our great pleasure to see Lydia – the woman who wasn't supposed to talk or walk again–dance with her new husband Glen.

PRIVATE MESSAGES TO A GRIEVING MOM

Norma's son Oscar took his life by a self-inflicted gunshot wound. Oscar was a Christian, but he had battled severe depression for years. At that time there was not as much help available to treat this disease as there is now.

Oscar and his mom enjoyed a remarkably close relationship. In those days, Norma carried a pager for her work as a home health nurse. Oscar would often send her a message with just the numbers "007", which was his secret code for "I love you and I'm okay." For about a week after Oscar's death, Norma received that secret message on her pager every morning.

For the next year, Oscar's favorite song would come on the radio in her car several times a week. Then, while going through some of Oscar's things, she found a photo of him that had been taken the year before he died while he was camping with friends. In the photo, he was laughing and leaping into the air, with the campfire in front of him. Above him was an image of an angel in a white robe with long hair. The image was clear enough to make out the facial features of the angel. All these messages comforted this mother's heart and confirmed that her son was indeed okay.

ANGEL BRINGS MESSAGE OF HOPE (name changed)

Rita was desperate. Four family members had passed away within a period of six weeks and Rita was begging the Lord for some relief. The grief and stress seemed too much to bear. She spent hours every day petitioning the Lord, finally telling Him in desperation, "If You are not going to take me to You, then You are going to have to come to me."

As Rita lay on her bed one morning, an angel appeared at the foot of the bed, glowing with a radiant blue light. She immediately felt enveloped in the peace of the Lord, fully secure and protected. The angel did not speak, yet somehow communicated the overwhelming love and goodness of God. Rita knew that the Lord had answered her prayers. She would be okay.

ANGELS UNAWARE

Angie remembers her angel encounter from years ago: "I was 19 and a new believer on a mission trip with the Baptist Student Union to hand out Bibles and bags of food to the homeless in the French Quarter of New Orleans, Louisiana. Our group walked up to three men who were sitting on a bench, looking like typical street bums, complete with brown paper bags.

"I just silently stood there, taking in the scene, while the leader of our group talked to the men about Jesus and told them there was a Bible in their bag of food. One of the men said, 'Oh, I know a Bible verse, but I don't know what it says.' He gave us the scripture reference, but we could not look it up because it was dark and that was before cellphones.

"As we were walking away, I heard the Lord speak to my spirit, telling me to turn around, go back, and hug the nastiest one of the men. I did not want to do it and resisted, but the urging would not go away. Finally, I said, 'Okay, I'll go; but if this is not You, at least I tried to obey You.'

"I did not tell anyone in my group. I just turned around and ran back over to the men in the dark. The one I was supposed to hug stood up. I hugged him, but I did not know what to say, except that I was supposed to hug him. He looked at me, smiled, and said, 'I'm proud of you.' I got chills, but I turned around and ran back to my group.

"That night my roommate and I looked up the scripture that the man had referenced. It was **Heb. 13:2**: *'Don't forget to show hospitality to strangers, for some who have done this have entertained angels without realizing it!'* I started crying because I immediately knew that he had been an angel."

MESSENGERS OF HEALING (name changed)

Franklin tells the story of his friend Cindy in Arkansas: Cindy was a feisty little lady–a transplant from Cajun country in Louisiana. Her doctor had ordered exploratory surgery to try to find the cause of some puzzling symptoms. This was fifty or sixty years ago, before some of the modern diagnostic scans were available. When the surgery was done, the doctor found her body so full of cancer that he only clamped the incision together; not even stitching it closed, because he was certain she would not live long enough for it to heal. They told her there was nothing they could do for her.

That night as she lay in her hospital bed, Cindy saw angels all around her bed and she felt the peace of God surround her as she fell asleep. The next morning when she awoke, she knew that she was totally healed. When the nurse came in to check on her, Cindy sat up in bed and announced, "I'm hungry. I want some red beans and rice."

The nurse blurted out, "You can't eat that. You're dying!"

Cindy responded, "No, I'm not. I'm healed."

And she was. Every year on the anniversary of her healing, Cindy returned to the hospital to celebrate with the staff and to remind them what God had done.

FROM HELL TO HOPE

Steven's irresponsible lifestyle had caught up with him. An overdose of drugs landed him in a Chicago hospital emergency room. As the medical team worked to save his life, Steven found himself suddenly outside his body. He could see the ER staff pumping his stomach on the table below him.

In an instant, he was transported to a dark, terrible place. He was suspended above a pit. The stench that rose from the pit was like that of thousands of dead bodies. He knew he was looking into hell.

Steven heard the screams of untold numbers of tortured souls as they begged for help. He could see hundreds of people trying to climb the slippery walls of the pit, only to be continually pulled back down by the others fighting for a way out. Try as they might, there was no escape. Steven could see it in their eyes. He could hear it in their screams. He could smell it and feel it.

Worse than the fear and the torment was the unrelenting hopelessness–the complete absence of the presence of God, with absolutely no way to get to Him. That was the reality of hell–never-ending eternity with no hope of love and no hope of grace–no hope at all.

Steven's heart was pounding in terror at the thought of being thrown into the pit. Just as he thought his heart would explode, he heard a voice say, "It's not your time."

The next thing he remembered was waking up the next day in a hospital room. A young African American boy was sitting in a chair beside his bed. The boy began to tell Steven about Jesus. He told him that Jesus loved him and wanted Steven to live his life for Him.

The little boy kept talking about Jesus until Steven's godparents came into the room. Steven asked them about the boy, but they just looked at him with a puzzled expression. They had not seen the boy who was talking to Steven as they came in. It could only have been an angel.

Although it took some time, Steven eventually did receive the message of hope brought by the angel that day. He trusted Jesus for salvation, so he will never have to worry about hell again. He married a beautiful Christian woman, and together they are sharing the good news that the angel brought to Steven that day: "Jesus loves you."

Lord, help us to discern and test every spirit. Make us receptive to every message from you, no matter what messenger you choose to send it–whether Holy Spirit, angel or human. Thank you for the angels all around us. In the powerful Name of Jesus. Amen.

Six

ANGELS OF PEACE AND PROVISION

Then the Devil went away, and angels came and cared for Jesus.
Matt. 4:11

IN THE PASSAGE ABOVE, WE SEE THAT ANGELS MINIStered to Jesus in the wilderness after He had been tempted by the devil following a forty-day fast. The Bible also gives examples of many other people receiving peace and provision from angels.

The angel of the Lord comforted Hagar in the desert and directed her to a well when she and Ishmael were about to die from lack of water (Gen. 21:17-19). Elijah also was ready to die in the desert, but an angel woke him up and gave him a hot meal and fresh water (1 Kgs. 19:3-8). When Jesus prayed in agony on the Mount of Olives, an angel came and strengthened Him (Luke 22:43).

In the gospel of Luke, Jesus tells of a poor beggar named Lazarus who suffered terribly in life. He lived in the street outside the door of a certain rich man's mansion. The rich man was uncaring and refused the poor beggar even a scrap of food. When Lazarus died, Jesus said he was carried by the angels to be with Abraham (Luke 16:22). But regarding the cold-hearted rich man, when he died, Jesus said his soul went to the place of torment. Sadly, there were no angel escorts for him.

What a blessing it is to know that our loved ones who trust in Jesus will have angels waiting to accompany them as they journey from this earthly realm to the heavenly one. Whether we see them or not, in our times of deepest need, God sends angels to be around us.

AN ANGEL LIGHTS THE WAY HOME

My husband Tom and I were both on the leadership team at our church's School of the Spirit, so we usually rode to the classes together, but one evening, Tom was unable to attend. After classes were over, I was moving my van closer to the front of the building to load some supplies when one of the students informed me that my passenger headlight was out. I was already a bit uncomfortable driving at night because my vision was not as clear in the dark, and a non-functioning headlight added to my uneasiness. I prayed, "Lord, you know that I don't see too clearly at night, and I really don't need to be driving without this light. I don't want to be a danger to myself or others. Please send an angel to make the light shine so I can see how to drive home. Thank you, Lord. Amen." Then I didn't give it another thought.

I loaded up my supplies and drove out onto the highway, praying in the Spirit, as I often do when driving alone. My goodness! My lights were the brightest they had ever been. I had plenty of light, even on the little country roads to my house. I never even used the high beams at all. I felt completely at ease. I just praised God all the way home. Then as I pulled into my garage, I could see the reflection of my headlights shining on the back wall – except there was only one reflection. The passenger headlight was still out! The angel hadn't repaired my light as I had thought, but he had provided light so I could see to drive home.

ESCORT ANGELS

As Shanna stood beside Isaiah's bed, she knew that her son was about to lose his battle with a disease that had wracked his young body with pain for years. He had fought bravely, but at any moment he would go to be with the Lord. Suddenly, two beautiful angels appeared—one on either side of Isaiah's hospital bed. They looked like ladies in white robes, shining with a brilliant white light. They did not speak, but they filled the room with peace. Shanna felt incredible peace and comfort as they stood gazing down at Isaiah while he took his last breaths. Then they were gone. She knew in her heart that they had come to escort her son to heaven.

ANGELS OF PEACE

Pamela was exhausted from the everyday concerns of parenting a child with special needs. She took a much-needed nap one day while her son was at school. She awoke feeling warm, relaxed and quite cozy. She could hear the most beautiful music, almost like someone humming a tune she had never heard. Pamela thought perhaps her husband had come home from work early. She heard the music slowly fade away until it was gone; then she rose from her bed and walked through the house. She called her husband's name, but he was not to be found. Only then did she realize that she had been visited by an angel. She felt wrapped in peace the rest of the day.

UNDER HIS WINGS (names changed)

Anna's daughter Joy had been in a bad vehicle accident. The doctors had not yet determined the full extent of her injuries and were keeping her heavily sedated until they could perform more tests the next day. Anna was exhausted from the stress and trauma of the day. Joy was a single mom and arrangements would have to be made for Joy's daughter to be cared for, as well as for someone to stay at the hospital with Joy.

Torn between fear of leaving her daughter for the night and the need to go home to sleep while Joy was sedated so she could return refreshed the next day, Anna closed her eyes and asked the Lord for guidance.

When she looked up from where she sat beside the door, she sensed the presence of an enormous angel in the room. Joy's bed was in front of her, and on the other side of it, Anna could see the angel's wings against the walls filling the entire room in a semi-circle that met at the door.

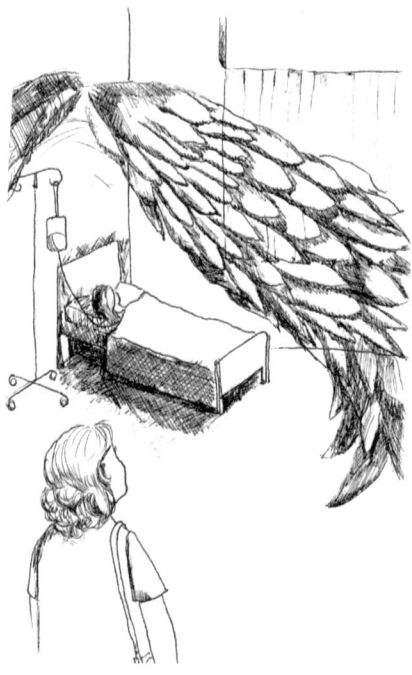

She could not see the body or the face of the angel–just the wings. But those wings–they were huge! She could see every detail–the individual feathers were an ivory color. Anna immediately thought of the scripture, ***"But for you who fear my name, the Sun of Righteousness will rise with healing in his wings."*** **Mal. 4:2**

Anna heard the Lord whisper, "She's fine. You can go." She knew He had given her permission to leave Joy in His loving care.

THE HOSPICE ANGEL

Don's mom Etta had been battling Myelodysplastic Syndrome for years and her body was no longer able to fight. Her care team at M D Anderson Cancer Center moved her to a nearby Hospice Center where she could be kept comfortable. Once the blood transfusions she had been receiving at the hospital were discontinued, her body would shut down in a day or two. So, Don and his two brothers, along with Etta's sister Barbara and Barbara's husband Roy, had come from their homes in different states to spend those remaining hours with the mother and sister they cherished so much.

Even though she was heavily sedated, Etta was still somewhat aware of what was going on around her. The second morning Don, Barbara and Roy were in the room when a nurse came in to administer morphine. When Etta heard morphine mentioned, she cried, "No, no, no!"

Don told the nurse not to give her the morphine. Soon, however, it became apparent that his mom was suffering, so Don went to the nurses' station and told the nurse he had made a mistake. He asked her to please give his mom the medication to ease her pain.

Feeling guilty for not following his mother's wishes, Don walked on past her room to an entrance area of the hospice building. No one was sitting in there when he walked in, but a young man and woman were playing pool on a billiards table in the open area of the room.

Don said, "For some reason, I sat down in the center of an empty sofa, not on one end as I normally would have done. Then I suddenly found myself in a conversation with a woman who was sitting next to me to my right. She was an elderly, grey-haired woman. There was nothing special about her. The conversation was about my mother. It didn't start out about the weather or anything and I never asked her name. She was asking extremely specific questions about my mother. I was bragging to this woman about how wonderful my mother was. At some point, she asked me, 'Do you think I could meet your mother?'"

Don said, "Sure!"

They immediately got up and walked to his mother's room.

Don described what happened next: "Looking in from the front door, there were two beds on the left that stuck out perpendicular from the wall. No one was in the first bed. My mother was in the second bed. Only my Aunt Barbara and her husband Roy were in the room at the time. I followed behind the lady as she walked over to my mother. She leaned over slightly, with her head bowed, and started praying over my mother. I couldn't hear what she was saying, but she was obviously praying.

"I was looking at this situation and my intellect was telling me that something was not right. I was confused and desperate to figure it out. I was looking at this woman and the only thing I could figure out was that, although she wasn't beautiful, her features were perfect. Her chin was pronounced, her nose was perfect; but, overall, she was not beautiful in any way. About that time, I realized what was going on.

"There was a nightstand between the two beds, with a lamp on the nightstand. The lamp was on and it cast a glow on the entire wall. The woman was standing between me and the wall, yet I could still see the entire wall–no shadow or anything. Just as I came to this realization, the woman finished praying for my mother. She stood up, looked at me, and she left. I felt that she didn't have time to reach the door, but she was gone.

"I immediately felt a strong urgency to talk to my mother, so I started telling her that I loved her and what a great mom she was. But this voice in my head said, 'No, tell her the rest of the story.' So, I began to tell her, 'Mom, I think Jesus has come for you, so if you see the light, go.' She was gone before I got the words out of my mouth. I was standing so close to her that I could feel it. The hair stood up on my arms. It was so powerful!"

A year later, Don was visiting family in Mississippi and had breakfast with Barbara and Roy. He asked them, "Do you remember the lady who came in and prayed for Mom right before she passed away?" They looked at each other curiously. Neither of them remembered seeing any lady come in to pray for her. It could only have been an angel.

ANGELS PROVIDE EMERGENCY WATER

Bobby and his son Josh are experienced hikers. They have tackled trails in the Canadian Rockies, the Grand Canyon, Arches and Zion National Parks. They have also hiked all the trails in the Great Smoky Mountains National Park. They always carry supplies of water, food, hammocks, bear spray, etc.

On a hot July day, Bobby and Josh set out on a hike in the Appalachian Mountains of Virginia. They were hiking the Dragon's Tooth Trail, which had an elevation of about 3700 feet. After hiking with an eighteen-pound backpack for about ten hours to the high elevation, seventy-year-old Bobby was beginning to tire. The temperature had soared higher than expected, and their water supply was nearly depleted. After leaving Dragon's Tooth, they had only eight ounces of water left between the two of them. They were still a few miles from the creek they were looking for and it was ninety-four degrees. As they rested, they watched for other hikers, knowing that they would be few and far between.

After a while, they saw a young couple approaching them on the trail. Bobby noticed that their hands were empty, and they did not have backpacks; but they were desperate, so he asked if they had any water. The young lady said that they did not have water and she asked if they were out. Bobby told her they only had their emergency water bottle left, and they had several more hours to hike to the creek to refill and filter more water. She said that she and her husband were Christians and asked if they could lay hands on Bobby and Josh and pray for them.

After they had prayed together, they talked for a few minutes. As they were talking, another young couple came walking up the trail. Bobby asked if they had water. The young man said, "How much do you need?" He opened a CamelBak and gave them two liters of water! They all laughed and told the couple that they had just prayed for water and God had answered almost before they had finished praying. The second couple said that they were Christians, too.

After Bobby and Josh left to finish their hike, they knew that they would see the two couples farther down the trail. The sun had gone down behind the mountains, and as daylight was fading they stopped at a camping area to wait for them because they had headlamps, and they had noticed that neither of the couples had any lights at all. There were still some treacherous, steep-sided trails ahead–too dangerous to navigate without lights. They waited for over an hour, but the two couples never came back.

Bobby and Josh had hiked a lot of miles before and they knew how hikers looked and smelled on those cross-country trails and those couples did not fit the bill. They did not wear hiking boots–only flip-flops and sandals. They did not have hiking equipment, trekking poles, or backpacks. How did they climb to 3700 feet on steep rocky inclines without proper footwear and gear and never break a sweat? Bobby and Josh both agreed that they were angels, sent by God to provide them with water.

HEAVENLY POWER

LaShawna's husband Steven had gotten paid today, but, unfortunately, he had not been able to leave work in time to get to the electric company to pay the overdue bill. He arrived home to see the electric company technician removing the meter box from the outside wall of his house.

Not looking forward to spending the night in the sweltering July heat with no air conditioning, Steven walked into the house to face his family.

But LaShawna was not about to have a pity party. She gathered the family for prayer, trusting God to take care of them. Then LaShawna and Steven decided to go get charcoal and have a cookout. They were on the way to the store when their daughter called and said, "Mom, the lights are back on!"

How could the lights be on? They had seen the man remove the meter box from the house when he disconnected the electricity. LaShawna and Steven turned around and went back home. Sure enough, the lights were on, the air conditioner was on, the stove, microwave, tv–everything worked–with no meter box on the house!

The next morning Steven went to pay the bill as soon as the electric company opened. They did not believe that he had electricity at his house with no meter box and no connection to the power source, but when the technician came to replace the box and turn the electricity back on, he had to admit that there had been some heavenly intervention. A Power Source bigger than the electric company had sent an angel of provision to turn on the lights!

Lord, you are my Provider. You use angels to deliver your provision when I cannot provide for myself. Thank you for taking care of my every need. I completely trust in you. In the amazing Name of Jesus! Amen.

Seven

Angels of Deliverance and Protection

For he orders his angels to protect you wherever you go.
Ps. 91:11

There is no question that the Lord commissions his angels to protect believers. An angel protected Daniel in the den of lions (Dan. 6:21-22). God rescued the kingdom of Judah by sending an angel to kill 185,000 Assyrian troops in one evening (2 Kgs. 19:35). The Lord sent an army of angels to protect the prophet Elisha and his servant from the Aramean army that had surrounded the city where Elisha lived (2 Kgs. 6:14-16).

When the apostles were arrested, an angel opened the gates of the jail cell and brought them out (Acts 5:18-19). When King Herod Agrippa had Peter arrested, the church prayed for him, and the Lord sent an angel to release him from his chains and bring him out of prison (Acts 12:5-10). An angel gave Paul a prophetic message that he and everyone on the ship on which he was sailing would be kept safe if they stayed with the ship (Acts 27:22-26).

Jesus warned people not to despise or harm children because their angels (plural, indicating there must be at least two per child) are always in God's presence (Matthew 18:10). But angels do not only guard and protect children. Angels are God's servants. They are spirit beings that He sends to help those who will receive salvation (Hebrews 1:14). Some of the most dramatic angel encounters have been those in which angels rescued humans from a dangerous situation. When we need to be rescued, God sends angels to be around us.

AN ANGEL PUSHES PAUSE

My husband Tom and I were on vacation in Arkansas. We always pray for extra angelic protection when we travel, and I am so glad that our Father provides. Tom was driving when we stopped for a red traffic light where the two-lane-road we were on intersected with a four-lane highway. There was almost no traffic as we waited for the light to change.

The light turned green and I glanced over at my husband. He was staring straight ahead. Everything was strangely still. I felt as if I were watching a scene from a movie that had been paused. I started to tell Tom that the light was green, but I heard a commanding voice say, "Be still." I kept quiet and did not move a muscle. Suddenly, a large semi- truck blew through the intersection from the left, running the red light and never even slowing down!

As soon as the truck passed, it was as if the "play" button had been pushed and everything was back to normal. Tom saw that our light was green and started driving across the intersection, completely unaware of our close call. It had all happened in a matter of seconds, but those few seconds on pause had saved our lives.

AN ANGEL TAKES THE WHEEL (names changed)

Gina and Trish were taking a group of youth from their church to a youth conference in Ridgecrest, South Carolina. They had stopped for a snack and restroom break and now Gina was attempting to re-enter the bumper-to-bumper interstate traffic.

As Gina crept along the entrance ramp watching for an opening, a car suddenly came up from behind the church van on the left side intending to force its way into traffic. There was nowhere for Gina to go to get out of the way. There was no room between them and the interstate traffic. They were about to be in the middle of a multi-vehicle collision.

One of the young girls in the van saw the car headed toward them and started screaming. Then–in an instant–they were out of the way! Gina looked at Trish and said, "I could feel a presence take over my hands on the wheel and my foot on the pedal. Then it was over."

Trish looked at her with wide eyes and said, "Oh."

Gina just repeated, "Oh."

They both knew that it could only have been an angel that saved them.

ANGELIC BODYGUARD

Jennifer was in San Francisco for business purposes. She parked in front of an office building to drop off some papers, not realizing she was parking in a tow-away zone. When she came out, she found that her car had been towed.

To make matters worse, she had locked her purse inside the car, so she did not have access to her identification, credit cards, or money. She had to walk to the nearest Western Union office, which was ten or twelve city blocks away, to have some money wired to her to get her car from the impound company.

The process took several hours, so when Jennifer got the money, she was anxious to get to the impound lot before they closed. She got directions and hurriedly set out on her way. Being unfamiliar with the city, she soon realized she had walked into a rough section of town. People were hanging out in doorways and standing in groups along the street, staring at her as she walked by. She was aware of how vulnerable she was–a young, professionally dressed woman, in heels, with money in her hand—but she had no idea how to get back to safety or to the impound lot. She sent up a quick prayer.

Then suddenly, a man fell in step beside her. Rather than fear, she felt relief. He seemed to be an older man, taller than her, wearing a blue cardigan. He somewhat reminded her of Mr. Rogers from the television show. She felt very safe and comfortable with him. She never saw his face because he told her not to look at him and not to look up, so she kept her head down. He walked beside her the entire time until they arrived safely at the impound lot. Then when she turned to thank him, he was gone. He had just vanished. Her angelic bodyguard had disappeared.

MOTORCYCLE ANGEL

Jeffrey was a young teenager, just enjoying riding his motorcycle on a logging road back in the woods on his family's property. The logging company had worn the old clay dirt road down until it was as slick as glass. Being a silly kid, Jeffrey was only wearing a pair of shorts and tennis shoes—no shirt, no helmet.

When he came around a curve at about twenty-five mph, the motorcycle went into a skid on the wet, slick clay. It was sliding directly toward a huge pile of logs on the side of the road–enough logs to load out a semi-truck. The first log was bigger than the front tire of the motorcycle–too big for Jeffrey to even reach around. Hitting the pile of logs would be like running into the side of a building!

As he slid, Jeffrey just closed his eyes and locked his arms. He thought, "Here it comes. I'm going to hit!" He was not sure what would happen, but he knew it would not be good.

It seemed like just a millisecond went by and the next thing Jeffrey knew, he was sitting right in the middle of the road, going the way he should have been going, eight to ten feet away from the logs. He was not giving the motorcycle any gas, but he was just sitting there with the engine idling and he was breathing really hard. How did he get there when he had been about to hit those logs? He had no idea. There was no earthly way.

AVOIDING THE TRAIN

Patricia had traveled this dark road at night several times a week for years. She was so familiar with it she could have driven it with her eyes closed. She knew there was a railroad crossing just around the next little curve, but never – not even once – had she seen a train cross there.

As usual, Patricia was caught up in a worship song as she was driving. When she came around the curve, right in front of her was a train bearing down fast on the crossing! She could see the terror in the Engineer's eyes as he saw that she was about to collide with the train. She was going too fast and she was too close to the track to stop.

In the next instant, Patricia found herself stopped, safely back from the train tracks. How did that happen? It had to be her angel.

LITTLE GIRL ANGELS (names changed)

For years Maggie had no idea that angels had saved her life. Her husband Derrick had been very physically abusive for most of their marriage, especially when he had been drinking. Maggie had taught her two little girls, Patty and Katie, ages four and three, to hide in the closet when Daddy came home in that condition. They were not to come out for any reason until she came to get them out, no matter what they heard going on in the house. That had become their routine.

One night, Derrick came home excessively intoxicated. Soon everything escalated and Patty took Katie into their closet hiding place. Derrick was a gun collector and that night he pulled out a snub nose shotgun. He shoved it into Maggie's throat so hard that she could not swallow or even breathe. He told her, "You are about to die."

Maggie was sure she *was* going to die. She even felt her spirit leave her body and rise over the living room. She could see the scene playing out before her. She could see Derrick and she could see herself. She could see everything, but she could hear nothing. There was just a deafening silence.

About that time Maggie saw Patty and Katie come out of the bedroom. Patty was holding Katie's hand. Maggie thought, "It is such a shame that my girls are going to have to see their mama die at the hands of their daddy."

Then Maggie was immediately back in her body. She could hear Patty and Katie pleading, "Daddy, please don't do this! Daddy, please don't kill Mama!" Derrick looked at the girls, then put down the gun and left the house.

Shaking uncontrollably–as soon as Maggie could catch her breath–without even thinking about it, she ran to the bedroom and pulled Patty and Katie out of the closet. She quickly put them in the car, and they drove away, never to spend another night in the house with Derrick.

Years later, when Patty and Katie were adults, Maggie and the girls were talking about their life with Derrick. Maggie finally had the courage to ask, "On that last night when your daddy had that gun to my throat and was about to kill me–on that one particular night–what made you girls come out of the closet?"

Patty said, "We didn't come out of the closet, Mom. You came and got us."

Maggie said, "Don't you remember? You came out and begged your daddy not to kill me."

Patty said, "No, Mom, we didn't come out of the closet until you came and got us out!"

That's when Maggie knew. It had been angels who had appeared in the form of her two little daughters, because they were the only ones who could have gotten through to her husband that night. Those "little girl" angels had intervened and saved her life.

ANGELS ALL AROUND US

Thank you, Lord God, that you give your angels charge over me. I ask you to charge them to protect and deliver me and my family from every attack and assignment of the enemy. Thank you for placing angels all around us. Sharpen my spiritual senses and give me discernment and wisdom. In the mighty Name of Jesus. Amen.

Eight

THE BUSINESS OF HEAVEN

I watched as thrones were put in place and the Ancient One sat down to judge.
Dan. 7:9

UP TO THIS POINT, WE HAVE LOOKED AT THE FAITHFUL angels and how they deliver comfort, healing, and provision from God. We have seen how they observe humans with wonder, especially during worship, even joining in on occasion. We have been amazed by the supernatural rescue missions that God has orchestrated to save his people from harm. Now we will look behind the scenes to see how business is conducted in heaven. We will also see what happened when some of the angels rebelled against God.

All angels were created to have fellowship with God and to serve and worship Him. The angels in the First Sphere (see Chapter Two) are continuously in the presence of God, praising Him and guarding His glory. There are also angels who meet with God in divine council (or assembly) meetings, where God presides over the meetings (Ps. 82:1; Ps. 89:5-7; 1 Kgs. 22:5-7; Job 1:6, 2:1). Depending on the translation you read, these angels may be referred to as angels, watchers, observers, sons of God, holy ones, sons of the Most High, or even gods (see other names for angels in Chapter 1).

This does not mean that angels are equal to Yahweh God or to Jesus the only begotten Son of God. The confusion comes from the Hebrew word *elohim,* which can be singular or plural, depending on context. It is one of those words that can be difficult to carry over into English. We find it translated not only as *angel,* but as both *God* and *gods.*

So, who or what is an *elohim*? Strong's Concordance defines it as "any person characterized by greatness or power." In other words, Yahweh God is *Elohim*. Angels are *elohim*. But angels are NOT Yahweh. Yahweh (Father, Son and Holy Spirit) is uniquely God (big "G"). He is all-powerful (omnipotent). He is all-knowing (omniscient). He is everywhere, all the time (omnipresent). And He is eternal (without beginning or end). These are attributes that cannot be ascribed to angels.

What does all this mean? God said, **"Look now; I myself am he! There is no god other than me!"** Deut. 32:39

But God also commanded, ***"Do not worship any other gods besides me. Do not make idols of any kind, whether in the shape of birds*** or *animals or fish. You must never worship or bow down to them, for I the LORD your God, am a jealous God who will not share your affection with any other god!"*

Ex. 20:3-4

God says there are no other gods, but he also says we are not to worship other gods. Is God contradicting Himself? Of course not! God is saying there are plenty of other *elohim* or spirit beings – angels, both faithful and fallen. Those are the little "g" gods that are NEVER to be worshiped; because compared to Yahweh–the one who created all those spirit beings– they are not gods! They don't even compare. Yahweh is the only *Elohim,* (big "G") God.

For who in all of heaven can compare with the LORD? What mightiest angel is anything like the Lord? The highest angelic powers stand in awe of God. He is far more awesome than those who surround his throne.

Ps. 89:6-7

As God's family in heaven, angels are sometimes referred to in the Bible as "sons of God." This does not mean that they are equal with Jesus. Angels are just *similar* to Jesus in that they are spirit beings. Jesus is the only begotten Son of God (John 3:16). He was in the beginning with God and is fully God (John 1:1-3). Angels are created beings, created by and for Christ, and are subject to Him (Col. 1:16; 1 Pet. 3:22).

Humans become sons and daughters of God when they accept Jesus as their savior and are born into God's family. They are adopted as legal children, receiving all the benefits of a child of God, and enduring any suffering that comes from being a part of His family. Angels do not enjoy this kind of family dynamic.

But to all who believed him and accepted him, he gave the right to become children of God.

John 1:12

So you should not be like cowering fearful slaves. You should behave instead like God's very own children, adopted into his family–calling him "Father, dear Father." For his Holy Spirit speaks to us deep in our hearts and tells us that we are God's children. And since we are children, we will share his treasures–for everything God gives to his Son, Christ, is ours, too. But if we are to share his glory, we must also share his suffering.

Rom. 8:15-17

DIVINE COUNCIL MEETINGS

When God holds a council or divine assembly meeting, He hears reports from angels who have been assigned to observe or watch over nations, regions, churches and even individuals. God gives them assignments and sometimes even listens to their ideas. God certainly doesn't need angels to carry out his work (neither does he need humans), but he is a God of relationship. He chooses to use both angels and humans for his purposes.

In 1 Kings we get a glimpse of a Divine Council meeting in which God is discussing the destruction of the wicked King Ahab.

Then Micaiah continued, "Listen to what the LORD says! I saw the LORD sitting on his throne with all the armies of heaven around him, on his right and on his left. And the LORD said, 'Who can entice Ahab to go into battle against Ramoth-gilead so that he can be killed there?'

There were many suggestions, until finally a spirit approached the LORD and said, 'I can do it!'

'How will you do this?' the LORD asked.

And the spirit replied, 'I will go out and inspire all Ahab's prophets to speak lies.'

'You will succeed,' said the LORD. 'Go ahead and do it.'

"So you see, the LORD has put a lying spirit in the mouths of your prophets. For the LORD has determined disaster for you." **1 Kgs. 22:19-23**

Amazingly, even after being told that his false prophets were lying, Ahab still listened to them and went into battle and was killed. The angel who suggested the strategy had obviously been observing Ahab long enough to be aware of his prideful heart. He knew that Ahab preferred to listen to those who told him what he wanted to hear, rather than what God was saying.

RESULTS OF ANOTHER COUNCIL MEETING

In the fourth chapter of Daniel, King Nebuchadnezzar was visited in a dream by a watcher angel who delivered a message of a coming judgment. This one was also due to pride.

Nebuchadnezzar was sentenced to spend seven years living as a wild animal in the fields, eating grass like a cow. The angel told the king that the judgment had been decreed by the watchers, commanded by the holy ones, and that the purpose of the decree was that the world would know that the Most High rules over the kingdoms of the world and gives them to anyone he chooses.

For this has been decreed by the messengers; it is commanded by the holy ones. The purpose of this decree is that the whole world may understand that the Most High rules over the kingdoms of the world and gives them to anyone he chooses – even to the lowliest of humans. **Dan. 4:17**

This was most likely the result of another divine council meeting from which an angel was dispatched to issue the decree to Nebuchadnezzar. Although the fulfilment of the decree would judge the king's pride, the higher purpose was to bring honor to God.

FALLEN ANGELS

As with humans, God gave angels free will. Some of the angels chose to rebel against God's authority. A certain group of angels rebelled against God's authority by manifesting in human bodies on earth and taking daughters of men as their wives.

But wait. Didn't Jesus say that the angels in heaven do not marry? Yes, He did, in Matthew 22:30. But Jesus was speaking of the angels who remained faithful to God in heaven. This group of unfaithful angels left their places in heaven to live on earth with human wives. The children produced from these unions were the giants (Nephilim) of Old Testament times.

When the human population began to grow rapidly on the earth, the sons of God saw the beautiful women of the human race and took any they wanted as their wives. ...In those days, and even afterward, giants lived on the earth, for whenever the sons of God had intercourse with human women, they gave birth to children who became the heroes

mentioned in legends of old.

Gen. 6:1-2. 4

This unnatural pairing of angels and humans unleashed unprecedented evil on the earth and the polluted human bloodline that resulted from these unions threatened the future Seed of Redemption that had been promised in the Garden of Eden. God responded to this corruption by cleansing the earth with a worldwide flood which destroyed all but eight people.

Noah was found righteous in God's eyes. Only he, his wife, his three sons and their wives survived the flood in the ark that God had Noah build. The angels who participated in this rebellion were bound in chains in darkness, to be kept there until the final judgment.

For God did not spare even the angels when they sinned; he threw them into hell, in gloomy caves and darkness until the judgment day.

2 Pet. 2:4

And I remind you of the angels who did not stay within the limits of authority God gave them but left the place where they belonged. God has kept them chained in prisons of darkness, waiting for the day of judgment.

Jude 1:6

Chief among fallen angels was one called Lucifer, who lusted after God's own throne and led an angelic rebellion.

How you are fallen from heaven, 0 shining star, son of the morning! You have been thrown down to the earth, you who destroyed the nations of the world! For you said to yourself, "I will ascend to heaven and set my throne above God's stars. I will preside on the mountain of the gods far away in the north. I will climb to the highest heavens and be like the Most High."

But instead, you will be brought down to the place of the dead, down to its lowest depth.

Isa. 14:12-15

He later became known as Satan (meaning *adversary* or *accuser)* or the devil. Adversary or Accuser is a title that is like our District Attorney. It is one who brings charges and makes a case against a defendant before a Judge in a court of law. The position, even in Bible times, was not a permanent one. In Job, we see Satan attending a Divine Council meeting while in the position of Accuser.

One day the angels came to present themselves before the LORD, and Satan the Accuser came with them. "Where have you come from?" the LORD asked Satan.

And Satan answered the LORD, "l have been going back and forth across the earth, watching everything that's going on." Job 1:6-7

WHAT HAPPENS TO SATAN AND THE REBELLIOUS ANGELS?

Satan and the fallen angels who followed him are cast out of heaven and thrown to the earth.

Then there was war in heaven. Michael and the angels under his command fought the dragon and his angels. And the dragon lost the battle and was forced out of heaven. This great dragon–the ancient serpent called the Devil, or Satan, the one deceiving the whole world–was thrown down to the earth with all his angels. Rev. 12:7-9

Our accuser has been defeated. His term is expiring, and he is not happy about it.

It has happened at last – the salvation and power and kingdom of our God, and the authority of his Christ! For the Accuser has been thrown down to earth–the one who accused our brothers and sisters before our God day and night. And they have defeated him because of the blood of the Lamb and because of their testimony. And they were not afraid to die. Rejoice, O heavens! And you who live in the heavens, rejoice! But terror will come on the earth and the sea. For the Devil has come down to you in great anger, and he knows that he has little time.

Rev. 12:10-12

As believers, we have an advocate (Jesus) pleading our case for us when the accuser brings any sin against us.

My dear children, I am writing this to you so that you will not sin. But if you do sin, there is someone to plead for you before the Father. He is Christ Jesus, the one who pleases God completely. 1 John 2:1

According to Jesus, at the Great Judgment at the end of the age, the rebellious angels will be cast into eternal fire.

In that day the LORD will punish the fallen angels in the heavens and the proud rulers of the nations on earth. They will be rounded up and put in prison until they are tried and condemned.

Isa 24:21-22

Then the King will turn to those on the left and say, "Away with you, you cursed ones, into the eternal fire prepared for the Devil and his demons!"

Matt. 25:41

Paul wrote to the church at Corinth: ***Don't you realize that we Christians will judge angels? So you should surely be able to resolve ordinary disagreements here on earth.***

1 Cor. 6:3

Perhaps the saints will have a part to play in judging the fallen angels and demonic spirits who instigated so much heartache and misery on the earth.

There are far more faithful angels than fallen ones (Rev. 12:3-4). Fallen angels are not privy to God's secrets plans and strategies. ***Why God doesn't even trust the angels.***

Job 15:15

Although they are powerful, fallen angels obviously did not retain *all* the power and glory they had when they dwelt in the presence of God. Faithful angels were able to bind fallen angels in chains and cast them into darkness to await the judgment. They were also able to defeat them and cast them out of heaven. Satan must *masquerade* as an angel of light because he no longer *is* an angel of light. ***Even Satan can disguise himself as an angel of light.***

2 Cor. 11:14

The devil and his angels are real. Do not take lightly their ability to hinder, oppress, and torment humans. It is wisdom to learn spiritual warfare and deliverance. But Christians who have been trained in spiritual warfare should not fear fallen angels or demons, because the Spirit of the living God dwells within the believer.

But you belong to God, my dear children. You have already won your fight with these false prophets, because the Spirit who lives in you is greater than the spirit who lives in the world.

1 John 4:4

TEST THE SPIRITS

There is only one gospel – the good news of eternal life through Jesus Christ. If you should ever encounter an angel who says anything that contradicts the Word of God or even hints that there is any other way to the Father besides Jesus, immediately tell that angel to leave in the Name of Jesus, because it will be a fallen angel or demon.

Even if an angel comes from heaven and preaches any other message, let him forever be cursed. **Gal. 1:8**

Jesus, you are King of Kings and Lord of Lords. At your Name, every knee will bow, and every tongue will confess that you are Lord, to the glory of God the Father! Father God, keep us from temptation and deliver us from every assignment and strategy of the evil one. In the glorious Name of Jesus. Amen.

Nine

Activating Angels

If you make the LORD your refuge, if you make the Most High your shelter, no evil will conquer you; no plague will come near your dwelling. For he orders his angels to protect you wherever you go. They will hold you with their hands to keep you from striking your foot on a stone.
Ps. 91:9-12

Angels are not God in any form: Father, Son or Holy Spirit. Nor do they do the things that only God can do. However, God uses these supernatural agents in numerous ways to carry out His purposes and to serve and assist mankind.

The missions of angels are diverse and endless. Angels often act as God's delivery service. Angels deliver messages of comfort and peace. They bring gifts of healing and miracles to believers. They do not save people, but there are salvation angels that help facilitate salvation by setting atmospheres and arranging circumstances and people in the right places at the right times. Angels are charged to protect and rescue humans. They guard children. They escort believers to heaven at death. They are assigned to individuals, churches, nations, and regions. They influence cultures and governments. They oppose demonic forces, plans and strategies.

Angels have demonstrated their incredible power as instruments of God's judgment numerous times in the past. Revelation informs us that angels will have this role again, carrying out the wrath of God in the last days. It's no wonder that we humans would have mixed feelings about encountering such magnificent creatures! These beings move easily between heaven and earth; from God's throne room to–well–our living room! What is the protocol for receiving such a visitor?

Most angel visitations are the "unaware" kind. Those are the ones in which the angels appear as humans and the people who encounter them do not realize that they have been in the presence of an angel until after the angel has vanished.

The next most common type of angel encounter involves one or more of the following: sensing an angelic presence; hearing a voice or voices speak or sing; hearing music with no known source; suddenly smelling a heavenly fragrance; seeing flashes of bright white or rainbow colored lights; or an invisible touch, like a hug or a hand that keeps you from falling.

None of the above encounters would require anything from you, other than to thank the Lord for sending angels to minister to you. I believe it is also appropriate (but not required) to say a simple "thank you" to any angel who is serving you. As a believer, you have angels assigned to serve and protect you. If you are in ministry, you probably have one or two extra ones. Our heavenly Father knows that we have an unseen enemy who puts a bullseye on our backs the moment we are saved. When we get to heaven, we may be surprised to learn how many times our angels have saved us from attacks of the one who seeks to steal from, kill, and destroy God's people.

CAN HUMANS ACTIVATE ANGELS?

Angels do not act on their own. They obey instructions or commands. They are subject to God–Father, Son and Holy Spirit. They act only according to His word. We can ask God to release angels of salvation or healing or worship into a ministry service. We can ask God to command angels to guard and protect us and our families. But can we activate or release angels ourselves? There has been much debate over this, so let's look at the authority of the believer.

Jesus came and told his disciples, "I have been given complete authority in heaven and on earth."

Matt. 28:18

He also said, *"And I have given you authority over all the power of the enemy, and you can walk among snakes and scorpions and crush them. Nothing will injure you."*

Luke 10:19

Jesus has complete authority over all the angels, both faithful and fallen. He has given this authority to those who believe in him. We are seated with Christ in the heavenly realms and are blessed with every spiritual blessing because we belong to Him. The same mighty power that raised Christ from the dead is available for those who believe in Him.

God *"has blessed us with every spiritual blessing in the heavenly realms because we belong to Christ."*

Eph. 1:3

I pray that you will begin to understand the incredible greatness of his power for us who believe him. This is the same mighty power that raised Christ from the dead and seated him in the place of honor at God's right hand in the heavenly realms. Now he is far above any ruler or authority or power or leader or anything else in this world or in the world to come. And God has put all things under the authority of Christ, and he gave him this authority for the benefit of the church. And the church is his body; it is filled by Christ, who fills everything everywhere with his presence.

Eph. 1:19-23

For he raised us up from the dead along with Christ, and we are seated with him in the heavenly realms–all because we are one with Christ Jesus.

Eph. 2:6

If we have the authority to command a fallen angel (a demon) to leave in the Name of Jesus why would we not have the authority to release a faithful angel in Jesus' Name to block demonic assignments when an alter call is given for salvation? Why could we not send an angel in the Name of Jesus to minister to a loved one in the hospital when no human visitors are allowed? Remember, angels will only act according to the word and will of God, so, of course we must not instruct them to do anything contrary to God's word or His will. They simply will not do it.

We also cannot expect angels to do for us those things which we should be doing for ourselves. But they are standing ready to help God's people with those things which He has purposed for them to do.

According to Ps. 139:16, God wrote a book about each of us, even before we were born. In those books are God's plans and purposes for our lives. Our angels assist us in carrying out these plans. They also protect us from the attacks and strategies of Satan and his angels.

God assigns angels to help us primarily with our spiritual callings. He also assigns angels to minister to our physical, financial, and emotional needs because they impact our ability to fulfill our spiritual missions.

HOW TO ACTIVATE ANGELS

First, be sure that your motive is pure. Never become fixated on seeing an angel, because by doing so you could open yourself to demonic activity. Angels are no substitute for a relationship with God. Angels are to minister to God's people. Seeing an angel does not mean that an individual is more spiritual or more holy than a person who does not.

Activating angels does not mean that you will necessarily see them. It just means that they will be released to minister more actively to you, according to God's plan for your life. You will, however, become more aware of their presence.

Since angels respond to the word and will of God, the best way I have found to activate angels is to pray or sing in the Spirit. When I pray or sing in tongues, I am sure that I am speaking God's word and His will. Angels hear it and they respond, often making their presence known. If you do not pray in tongues, then pray the word of God in your own language. God will honor your heart.

Sometimes angels appear to people for the purpose of delivering a message from God. Angels usually deliver their messages and are not prone to chat. There are exceptions, though. The angel might answer a question, if asked. Some people want to know the names of their angels. They might tell you, or they might not. Angels will only give information that God allows them to give.

If you do see an angel, remember that this is a spirit being who has access to the courts of heaven, and he or she deserves respect and honor. This is an immensely powerful being who is on orders from the King of Kings. Do not worship him; but respect him! There are angels all around us. It is just one of the ways that our Father God planned to care for his people from the beginning. Isn't our God amazing?

I praise you, God, for all the ways you love and care for me. Thank you for assigning angels to assist me throughout my life. Give me eyes to see your glory, for you are the One I worship and adore. In Jesus' Name. Amen.

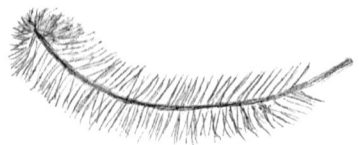

Ten

Heaven on Earth

Pray like this: Our Father in heaven, may your name be honored. May your Kingdom come soon. May your will be done here on earth, just as it is in heaven.
Matt. 6:9-10

The whole world has become the kingdom of our Lord and of his Christ, and he will reign forever and ever.

Rev. 11:15

It seems Jesus was always talking about the Kingdom. "The Kingdom of God is like", "the Kingdom of God belongs to", or "the Kingdom of God is near". Jesus instructed his disciples to pray for the Kingdom to come. In Matt. 12:28 and Luke 11:20, Jesus told those who accused him of casting out demons by the power of Satan, that because he cast demons out by the Spirit of God, it indicated that the Kingdom of God had arrived among them.

All believers are part of that Kingdom. No matter how things may appear, if we look with eyes of faith into the realm of the Spirit, we will see that Jesus is still seated at the right hand of the Father, with full power and authority over all creation and every living thing. As citizens of the Kingdom, we are to be about Kingdom business. God's angels are assigned to assist us in these endeavors.

But we will not just encounter angels in this age. We will have angels all around us for eternity! Jesus, the King of Kings and Lord of Lords – the King of all the angels and all the humans and all creation – is coming back to take His Bride (all believers in Christ) to live with Him in heaven. This will be the First Resurrection, when the bodies of those who died as believers in Christ will be resurrected and taken up to heaven, and those believers who are alive will be taken up into the clouds to meet the Lord. This event is also called the Rapture (meaning the *catching away*) by Christians today. Jesus will be shouting a command for the dead to rise and the living believers to "Come up here!"; an archangel will be calling out; and God will be blowing a trumpet! It will be quite a noisy affair – heard all over the world!

For the Lord himself will come down with a commanding shout, with the call of the archangel, and with the trumpet call of God. First, all the Christians who have died will rise from their graves. Then, together with them, we who are still alive and remain on the earth will be caught up in the clouds to meet the Lord in the air and remain with him forever.

I Thess. 4:16-17

This book is not a teaching about end-times events, so I will not get into all the details of the different views about the timing of the rapture, the possible identities of people, nations and locations in Daniel and Revelation, and I will certainly not set any dates for Jesus' return. Not even the angels know the day, and they will be right in the thick of it. One thing is for sure. We are closer today than we were yesterday. So be ready.

After the seven years of tribulation on the earth (you do not want to be here for that, so get right with God now), Satan and his demons will cause the rulers of the world to gather for battle against the Lord. Jesus will return to the earth, along with angels and resurrected saints. The

Lord's enemies will be quickly defeated, and Satan will be bound in chains in the bottomless pit for one thousand years. During that thousand years, King Jesus will rule the earth in peace, along with the resurrected saints and angels.

At the end of the thousand years, Satan will be released for a short time. He will deceive the nations again to come up for war against God. This time fire will fall from heaven and consume the attacking armies. Then Satan will be thrown into the lake of fire to be tormented day and night forever, along with all the rebellious angels who followed him. According to Jesus, at the Great Judgment at the end of the age, unbelievers will also be cast into eternal fire. This is for those who willfully rejected the gift of salvation through Jesus.

Then the King will turn to those on the left and say, "Away with you, you cursed ones, into the eternal fire prepared for the Devil and his demons!"

Matt. 25:41

But it is not God's will that any should perish. He sent his Son Jesus into the world so that all who believe in Him will be saved (John 3:16). God has a much better plan for humanity than we could ever imagine.

NEW HEAVENS AND A NEW EARTH

For the saints of God, eternity will be glorious. God has promised new heavens and a new earth! The capitol city of the universe will be New Jerusalem, which will come down out of the new heavens and sit on the new earth. The city will be 1400 miles wide, 1400 miles long and 1400 miles high. There will be no night there – no sickness or death – no pain or tears! There we will live forever with our Lord and Savior. And guess who our neighbors will be? The redeemed saints, of course; but also, angels!

No, you have come to Mount Zion, to the city of the living God, the heavenly Jerusalem, and to thousands of angels in joyful assembly. You have come to the assembly of God's firstborn children, whose names are written in heaven. You have come to God himself, who is the judge of all people. And you have come to the spirits of the redeemed in heaven who have now been made perfect.

Heb. 12:23

Imagine it. Eternity–forever with the Lord. All the redeemed saints of all the ages will be there–as will all the myriads of faithful angels – angels all around us.

Thank you, Father God, for the sure promise of a glorious eternity with you, through the blood of your Son, Jesus. I look forward to the time when I will live with you, along with all the saints and angels in the new heavens and new earth. While I remain on this earth, my prayer is that I will bring honor to Your name and sons and daughters to Your kingdom. Give me boldness to walk in the knowledge of my position as a child of God. Thank You for placing angels all around me. In the matchless Name of Jesus. Amen.

List of Contributors

Shanna Brady lives in Mississippi and is an Avon Representative. She loves to find a good bargain, so her job at a thrift store is a perfect fit for her. She also enjoys fishing and going to auctions.

Laurie Hilton Cason was born on the $4^{th \text{ of July}}$. While growing up in rural Mississippi, she was strongly influenced by the local county nurse, which led her to earn a degree in nursing. Laurie has provided nursing care to patients locally, nationally and in several European countries. She currently works in geriatrics, but she is looking forward to retirement and enjoying more time camping, fishing, playing outdoors, and spending time with her family and friends. She and her husband live in Waynesboro, Mississippi.

Retha Clements lives in Laurel, Mississippi, where she coordinates the annual Jones County March for Jesus. She is an ordained Elder in the Presbyterian Church, a children's minister, and a member of an intercessory prayer group. She enjoys shopping, traveling, and reading.

Norma Curby lives in Meridian, Mississippi. She is a nurse with a hospice service. She is of the Catholic faith. Some of her favorite activities are working with her flowers and sitting on her porch watching the ducks, but what she loves best is spending time with her grandchildren.

Pamela Creel lives with her husband and son in Richton, Mississippi. They attend a nondenominational church. Pamela is a stay-at-home mom. The family enjoys working together in their yard, walking, fishing, camping, and taking care of their pets.

Don Hammond is the owner of Hammond Electric. He loves the outdoors and enjoys hunting near Lake Okeechobee south of Orlando, where he is a partner in a hunting lease. Don lives in Miami, Florida.

Bobby Johnson is retired after 38 years of service in law enforcement on the local, county and state levels. He has traveled to 42 states, riding motorcycles cross country and hiking mountain trails throughout the nation. He loves snow skiing and ocean cruises, and he once did commercial deep-sea fishing for several months. He lives in Sandersville, Mississippi.

Patricia Jones is an excellent cook, decorator, and organizer. She has two children and two grandchildren. She loves reading and studying the word of God. Patricia is a passionate worshipper, seer, and intercessor whose goal is for people to know Jesus more intimately. She lives in Hattiesburg, Mississippi.

Angie Matheny stays busy as a mom and fulltime caregiver to her son Hunter. She enjoys reading as well as writing poetry and song lyrics. She and her son reside in Waynesboro, Mississippi.

Jeffrey Morrison and his wife live in Guntersville, Alabama, where he is a lumber broker and is President of American Lumber and Plywood. He also sells custom hangers for clothing. He enjoys spending time with his six beautiful children and one wonderful granddaughter. He loves fitness, sports, and flying.

Jennifer Morrison lives in Semathor, in South Australia, which is near Adelaide. She is a graphic designer and proud mom to two fur babies Jackson and Garcia.

Freeman Oglesby and wife Donna live in Laurel, Mississippi. He is a WW2 veteran and is retired from the poultry industry. In his nineties, Freeman still works out at the gym every day except Sunday.

LIST OF CONTRIBUTORS

Trina Overland is a well-known Bible teacher and piano teacher in Jones County, Mississippi. She taught private piano lessons for 30 years, as well as church choir. She has taught on the mission field, at conferences, city-wide Bible studies, home churches, and many other events, to groups of all ages. She enjoys crafts, growing flowers, tea parties, and cooking and decorating for family gatherings. She also likes travel, especially cruises.

Lydia Palmisano is retired and lives with her husband Glen in Stringer, Mississippi. She loves the Word of God, beautiful country and spending time with friends and family. She especially enjoys being with five-year-old granddaughter Emma, who lives with them. Lydia says she looks and acts like the daughter she lost in the traffic accident.

Steven and LaShawna Peppers live in Laurel, Mississippi and are the founders of Overcomers Ministries. Through the ministry they host outreach events throughout the area to share the gospel, meet needs, and promote unity among believers. They are sought-after speakers for conferences and events. Steven also does standup comedy routines and has been a contestant on the television show *Family Feud*. They are devoted to their family.

Scott and Marla Schiele are the founders of Outpouring International. They love traveling the world, equipping the body of Christ, and encouraging pastors and their families. They have four grown children who love to minister alongside them. The Schieles have pastored churches in Mississippi and Oklahoma, and now reside in Montana.

Ric Wright is the founder of Resurrection Lifestyle Ministries in Glasgow, Kentucky. Ric is an evangelist, revivalist, and speaker who brings resurrection life to wherever Jesus leads him. He brings energy, passion, and renewal wherever he is asked to share the "Good News." To book Ric for an event or conference, go to resurrectionlifestyle.org.

About the Author

Kay Hilton is a life-long student and teacher of the Bible. She is an ordained minister and is currently an online student of Israel Bible Center. She speaks and trains at conferences and events in the areas of Spiritual Gifts and Ministry, and Jewish Culture and Roots in Christianity. Her mission is to invite others into the Kingdom of God and to help them discover and develop their spiritual gifts. She enjoys reading, quilting, and making jewelry. Kay also loves spending time with her family and friends. She has a son and a daughter and six amazing grandchildren. She lives in Laurel, Mississippi with her husband Thomas.

Facebook Kay Hilton – Author Email
kayhilton.author@yahoo.com

About the Illustrator

Julie Banks is an artist in multiple media. In addition to painting and drawing, she makes beautiful, Spirit-inspired worship banners and flags. She is an excellent seamstress, cook and decorator, and is passionate about the ministry of deliverance and inner healing. She wants to see the members of the body of Christ learn who they are and embrace the talents and gifts God has given to each one. Julie is the mother of three daughters and grandmother of nine wonderful grandchildren. She and her husband Bobby live in Moselle, Mississippi.

www.ingramcontent.com/pod-product-compliance
Ingram Content Group UK Ltd.
Pitfield, Milton Keynes, MK11 3LW, UK
UKHW041954230426
12048UKWH00008B/339